ANCIENT CIVILIZATIONS
The
Incas

by Anita Ganeri

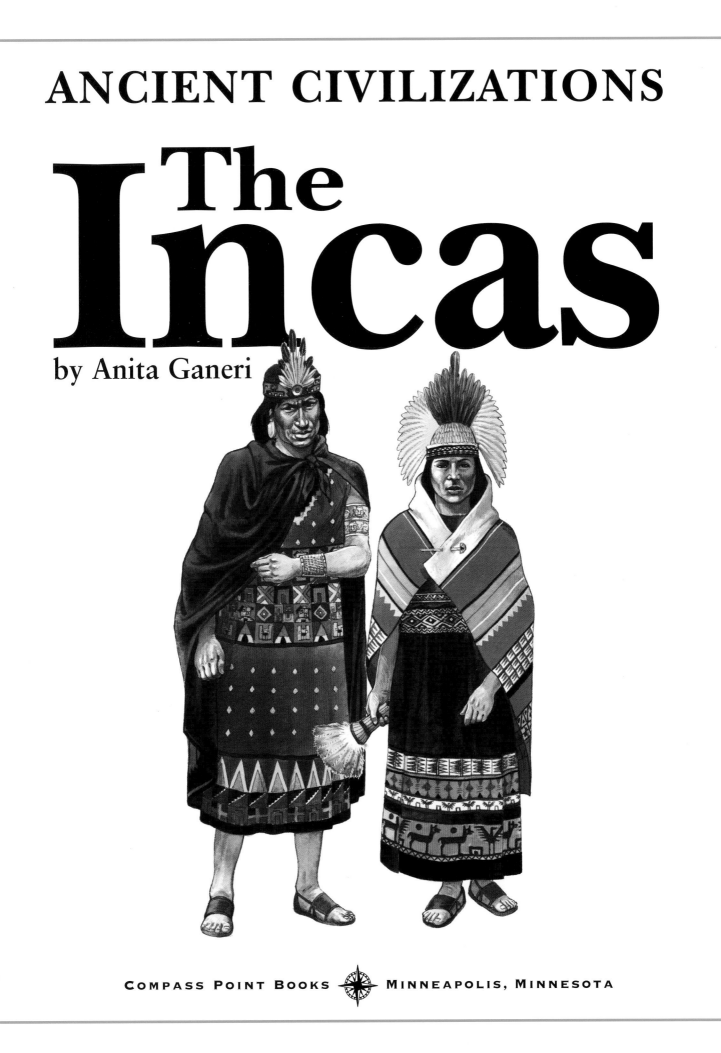

COMPASS POINT BOOKS ✦ MINNEAPOLIS, MINNESOTA

First American edition published in 2007 by
Compass Point Books
151 Good Counsel Drive
P.O. Box 669
Mankato, MN 56002-0669

THE INCAS
was produced by
David West Children's Books
7 Princeton Court
55 Felsham Road
London SW15 1AZ

Printed in the United States of America in North Mankato, Minnesota
122009
005654R.

Illustrator: Terry Riley
Designer: Rob Shone
Editors: Kate Newport, Robert McConnell
Page Production: Ellen Schofield and Bobbie Nuytten
Content Adviser: Robert J. Sharer,
  Shoemaker Professor in Anthropology,
  University of Pennsylvania Museum

Visit Compass Point Books on the Internet at
www.compasspointbooks.com
or e-mail your request to
custserv@compasspointbooks.com

Library of Congress Cataloging-in-Publication Data
Ganeri, Anita, 1961-
  The Incas / by Anita Ganeri.—1st American ed.
    p. cm.—(Ancient civilizations)
  Includes bibliographical references and index.
  ISBN-13: 978-0-7565-1951-3 (hardcover)
  ISBN-10: 0-7565-1951-9 (hardcover)
  ISBN-13: 978-0-7565-1953-7 (paperback)
  ISBN-10: 0-7565-1953-5 (paperback)
  1. Incas—History—Juvenile literature. 2. Incas—Social life and customs—
Juvenile literature. I. Title. II. Series: Ancient civilizations (Minneapolis,
Minn.)
F3429.G36 2006
985'.01—dc22   2006002992

Contents

The Incas

The Inca civilization of South America was centered on the Andes Mountains and was at its peak about 700 years ago. More than a million people lived under the rule of the Inca empire, and the Incas controlled a vast territory, ranging from Ecuador to northern Chile. The Inca capital was the city of Cuzco, in Peru. Although the Incas lived many years ago, we know a lot about them.

Look out for this man digging up interesting items from the past, like this engraved gold cup.

Who Were the Incas?

Little is known of the early history of the Incas. They were originally a small group of people who lived in southern Peru. About 800 years ago, they began to expand their rule, and over the next 200 years, they conquered many neighboring lands.

The first Inca people lived in small stone or mud-brick huts. They grew crops in the river valleys or on terraced fields in the mountains. They also raised flocks of llamas.

We know a great deal about the Inca civilization from artifacts, such as silver animal figurines.

The Incas were not the first people to settle in the area. Many other civilizations came before them. The Moche people lived on the northern desert coast of Peru nearly 500 years earlier. They were highly skilled potters, goldsmiths, and weavers.

Another civilization, the vast Chimu empire, lasted from about 1150 to 1450. Its capital was the mud-brick city of Chan Chan in northern Peru. The Chimus were later conquered by the more powerful Incas.

The Inca World

The Inca empire covered a large area of South America, stretching for about 2,500 miles (4,023 kilometers) along the west coast. It included parts of the modern-day countries of Peru, Ecuador, Bolivia, Argentina, and Chile. The lands ruled by the Incas included many types of climates and landscapes.

Moche clay figure

Quito •

Amazon River

Chan Chan
• Moche

• Chavin
Paracas •

Machu Picchu

Machu Picchu
• • Cuzco
Nazca •
Lake Titicaca
Tiahuanaco •

PACIFIC OCEAN

ANDES MOUNTAINS

Lake Titicaca

The Inca Empire

Inca Empire

When an Inca killed an enemy soldier, he usually made his victim's teeth into a necklace. The skull was dipped in gold and made into a grisly drinking goblet.

Amazon rain forest

The red lines on the map show the amazing network of roads built by the Incas to link the parts of the empire.

Royal Inca roads

Centered on the mighty Andes Mountains, the longest mountain range in the world, the Inca empire also included dry coastal deserts and lush, tropical rain forests. It was a difficult land for the Incas to live in, but that did not stop the empire from expanding very quickly.

The Incas conquered their empire by force. The army was well trained and highly organized, and it was often led into battle by the emperor himself. Soldiers were mostly farmers who served in the army as part of the tax they owed to the emperor.

Manco Capac and Mama Ocllo

Lake Titicaca lies high in the Andes Mountains. For the Incas, the lake was a holy place. They believed it was where their ancestors first came to Earth. Long ago, the great god Viracocha created the first people out of clay. He breathed life into them and sent them down to Earth to live amid the lakes, caves, and hills. The world was still in darkness, so Viracocha ordered the sun, moon, and stars to rise from Lake Titicaca into the sky. But the first people ran wild, and Viracocha did not like what he saw. So Inti, the sun god, sent his two children to Earth. They were Manco Capac and his sister, Mama Ocllo.

Inti gave them a golden rod and told them to prod the ground. When they found a place where the rod sank into the ground, he said, this is where they should build a great city.

Manco Capac and Mama Ocllo came to Earth on Lake Titicaca, on the Sacred Island of the Sun. Then they headed north until they came to a place where the golden rod sank into the ground. This is where they built the city of Cuzco, which became the great capital of the Incas. People came from far and wide to the City of the Sun. There the children of the sun taught them how to weave, farm, build, make pots, and fight.

Ruling the Inca Empire

The Sapa Inca lived a life of great luxury. He was carried around on a golden throne and wore symbols of power, including a headdress made from the finest vicuña wool.

The Inca ruler was called the Sapa Inca, which means "the only emperor." He was believed to have descended from the sun god and was worshipped as a god. The Sapa Inca controlled everyone and everything in the empire. His word was law and had to be obeyed without question. The Sapa Inca ruled his vast empire very strictly, with the help of government officials.

People who broke the law were harshly dealt with in Inca times. A minor offense might only bring a public scolding. But for a serious crime, like laziness, the punishment was death.

Government officials were noblemen. The highest-ranking came from royal families, and they enjoyed a privileged position in Inca society. Below them, another group of nobles helped the emperor to govern newly conquered lands.

When an Inca emperor died, his body was mummified, or preserved. The royal mummies were paraded through the streets at special festivals.

Inca Builders

The Incas were very skillful builders. Their most famous buildings were made from blocks of stone. Stonemasons chipped the stones into shape using very simple tools. Then the blocks were dragged into place. Large buildings, such as temples, took years to finish.

The blocks of stone in an Inca wall fit together perfectly, even without cement. It was impossible to drive even the thinnest knife blade between the blocks.

The Incas built their capital, Cuzco, in a high mountain valley. The city was shaped to look like a crouching puma and was home to about 100,000 people. In the center of the city was the sacred square, which contained the great Temple of the Sun. Only the royal family and Inca nobles were allowed to live inside the city.

Cuzco was guarded by a massive stone fortress called Sacsahuaman. It was built into the steep hillside and had huge walls about 60 feet (18 meters) high to keep invaders out.

The sacred Inca city of Machu Picchu was built about 8,200 feet (2,500 m) up in the Andes Mountains in Peru. Hidden for many centuries, it was rediscovered by an American named Hiram Bingham in 1911.

Travel and Trade

An extraordinary network of roads linked all the parts of the Inca empire. About 10,000 miles (16,000 km) of roads were built, often across difficult ground. In the mountains, roads zigzagged up and down the steep slopes. The main highway was the Royal Road from Cuzco to Quito. Many of the travelers on the Inca roads were merchants.

Where roads had to cross deep valleys and ravines, the Incas built amazing rope bridges. These were regularly checked and inspected to make sure they were in good working order.

Teams of messengers traveled in relays all over the Inca empire, carrying messages for the emperor. Each runner blew a conch shell to warn the next runner in his team that he was on his way.

Incas traveled to local markets to trade goods such as llama wool for salt, shells, and birds' feathers. The Incas did not use money but usually bartered for goods. Most of the trade in Inca times was strictly controlled by the government.

The Incas did not have wheeled transportation, and they used llamas to carry heavy loads. Boats and rafts were used on lakes and rivers and along the coast.

Gods and Goddesses

Gods played a very important part in Inca life. The Incas' chief god was Viracocha, the creator, who made the world and the first people. But the most powerful god was the sun god, Inti. His wife was Mamaquilla, the moon goddess. Many places were believed to be sacred, including temples, lakes, and mountains. These places were called *huacas*. The holiest was the Temple of the Sun in Cuzco.

At festivals held in honor of the sun god, the emperor himself led the prayers and made offerings of food. Llamas were also sacrificed to the gods.

Apart from their religious duties, Inca priests also acted as doctors. To treat patients, the priests used many magic spells and charms, such as stones taken from a tapir's stomach.

The Incas held many religious festivals to honor their gods during the year. At these festivals, the priests made offerings of food and sacrificed animals to please the gods. The Incas were very superstitious. They would not do anything important without asking the priests to consult the gods for their advice.

The Inca emperors were believed to be descended from the sun god, Inti.

Growing Up

Life in an Inca family depended on whether the family was rich or poor, but all Inca children were brought up strictly. The sons of noblemen might have a tutor, but most children did not go to school. They were taught all they needed to know by their parents. From an early age, they were expected to help their parents in the house or fields and were kept very busy. Boys and girls were thought to reach adulthood when they were 14 years old. This is when a boy received his adult name and a loincloth at a special ceremony. A naming ceremony also was held for girls.

Most Inca people lived in simple houses made from mud bricks and thatched with grass. They had no real furniture but sat and slept on reed mats or woolen blankets.

An Inca girl got married when she was about 12 to 14 years old. Her husband was chosen by her parents. At a simple ceremony, the bride and groom held hands and exchanged sandals.

*Instead of writing, the Incas used **quipus** to send messages and keep records. A quipu was made from lengths of knotted string. Its colors and knots had meanings.*

Clothes and Jewelry

Inca clothes were usually very simple. Men wore long, sleeveless tunics over a loincloth. Women wore ankle-length dresses tied at the waist with a sash. Over the top, they wore cloaks or shawls. Leather or grass sandals covered their feet. In warmer places, clothes were made from cotton. In the cooler mountains, they were made from warm llama wool.

Inca men carried small woolen bags, slung over a shoulder, underneath their cloaks. In the bags, they carried good luck charms, or amulets.

A noble's clothing

Inca nobles dressed in a style similar to that of ordinary people, but their clothes were made from much better quality materials. They were also beautifully decorated with tiny gold beads or brightly colored feathers from rain forest birds like parrots and macaws.

The finest clothes and jewelry were reserved for the Sapa Inca himself. He was so important that he wore new clothes every day.

Sapa Inca clothing

Noble Incas wore large ear plugs made from gold and inlaid with precious stones. The more important the person, the bigger and finer the ear plugs.

Arts and Crafts

From golden statues of the gods to pots for everyday use, Inca craft workers produced many beautiful objects. Craft workers were highly respected and valued. They were excused from paying taxes to the emperor, and they were provided with everything they needed. Weaving was perhaps the most important craft. Cloth was made from wool and cotton, dyed in bright colors. The Incas were also skilled metalworkers, making huge quantities of exquisite jewelry, statues, and masks from gold and silver. All the gold and silver belonged to the emperor.

Most cloth was woven on a backstrap loom. One end of the loom was tied to a post or tree trunk. The other end of the loom had a strap that went around the weaver's back.

Inca potters did not use a potter's wheel. They made pots from coils of clay. Then they painted or carved decorative patterns.

Some craft workers made stunning cloaks from the feathers of tropical birds. These were only worn by the highest-ranking of the Inca nobles.

Farming and Food

Much of the land in the Inca empire was mountainous and difficult to farm. Farmers cut steps into the hillside to make the fields level enough to grow crops. The soil was held in place by stone walls, and special ditches were dug to bring water to the fields. Crops included maize, or corn, potatoes, beans, and cotton. Farmers also kept llamas and alpacas and grazed them on the high mountain grasslands. Ducks and guinea pigs were also raised for food.

The Incas used maize to make chicha, *a very strong drink. It was enjoyed on special occasions and offered to the gods at festivals.*

A favorite Inca dish was corn cooked with other vegetables and spices. Corn was also ground into flour and used to make flat bread. Only the wealthiest Incas could afford to eat fish and meat regularly.

Farmers grew different crops at
different levels of the hillside. This
meant they would not starve
if one crop failed.

What Happened to the Incas?

By the end of the 15th century, the Inca empire had reached the height of its power. But when the emperor Huayna Capac died, a bloody civil war broke out between the rival followers of his two sons. Eventually, Huayna's elder son, Atahualpa, won the throne.

An Inca kero, or wooden cup, shows the arrival of Francisco Pizarro and his Spanish forces in Peru.

Although the Spanish tried to destroy all traces of the Incas, they failed. Many people in Peru still follow Inca customs. They also speak Quechua, a version of the Inca language.

In 1532, Spanish soldiers arrived in the empire, led by Francisco Pizarro. The Spanish were greedy for Inca gold. Pizarro seized the emperor and held him for ransom. The emperor paid the ransom with a room filled with gold and another filled twice with silver. But despite receiving the ransom, Pizarro killed the emperor and set about destroying the once-mighty Inca empire.

Glossary

bartered—traded by exchanging goods, not by using money

chicha—a strong Inca drink

ear plugs—large earrings worn like studs through the ears

empire—a large state made up of many countries, all ruled by a leader called an emperor

huacas—sacred places

llamas—woolly haired South American animals that are related to the camel

loincloth—clothing worn by Inca men, made from strips of cloth tied around their waists and passed between their legs

puma—a large brown cat; also called a cougar or mountain lion

ransom—a demand for money or goods in return for releasing a captive

sacrificed—killed to honor the gods

Sapa Inca—the title given to the Inca emperor

stonemasons—skilled workers who build with stone

superstitious—fearing the unknown and believing in omens and the supernatural

thatched—covered with plant material

vicuña—a South American animal, similar to a llama

Further Resources

AT THE LIBRARY

Calvert, Patricia. *The Ancient Inca*. New York: Franklin Watts, 2004.

Lourie, Peter. *Lost Treasure of the Inca*. Honesdale, Pa.: Boyds Mills Press, 1999.

Rees, Rosemary. *The Incas*. Des Plaines, Ill.: Heinemann Library, 1999.

ON THE WEB

For more information on *The Incas*, use FactHound to track down Web sites related to this book.

1. Go to *www.facthound.com*
2. Type in this book ID: 0756519519
3. Click on the *Fetch It* button.

FactHound will find the best Web sites for you.

LOOK FOR MORE BOOKS IN THIS SERIES

ANCIENT CHINESE
ISBN 0-7565-1647-1

ANCIENT EGYPTIANS
ISBN 0-7565-1645-5

ANCIENT GREEKS
ISBN 0-7565-1646-3

ANCIENT MAYA
ISBN 0-7565-1677-3

ANCIENT ROMANS
ISBN 0-7565-1644-7

THE AZTECS
ISBN 0-7565-1950-0

THE VIKINGS
ISBN 0-7565-1678-1

Index